May 2019

DARING AND DANGEROUS

DEEP SEA DIVERS

SHERRY HOWARD

Education

rourkeeducat

Before, During, and After Reading Activities

Before Reading: Building Background Knowledge and Academic Vocabulary

"Before Reading" strategies activate prior knowledge and set a purpose for reading. Before reading a book, it is important to tap into what your child or students already know about the topic. This will help them develop their vocabulary and increase their reading comprehension.

Questions and activities to build background knowledge:
1. *Look at the cover of the book. What will this book be about?*
2. *What do you already know about the topic?*
3. *Let's study the Table of Contents. What will you learn about in the book's chapters?*
4. *What would you like to learn about this topic? Do you think you might learn about it from this book? Why or why not?*

Building Academic Vocabulary
Building academic vocabulary is critical to understanding subject content.
Assist your child or students to gain meaning of the following vocabulary words.
Content Area Vocabulary
Read the list. What do these words mean?

- *amputate*
- *bayonet*
- *disoriented*
- *narcosis*
- *perilous*
- *toxin*

During Reading: Writing Component

"During Reading" strategies help to make connections, monitor understanding, generate questions, and stay focused.
1. *While reading, write in your reading journal any questions you have or anything you do not understand.*
2. *After completing each chapter, write a summary of the chapter in your reading journal.*
3. *While reading, make connections with the text and write them in your reading journal.*
   a) *Text to Self – What does this remind me of in my life? What were my feelings when I read this?*
   b) *Text to Text – What does this remind me of in another book I've read? How is this different from other books I've read?*
   c) *Text to World – What does this remind me of in the real world? Have I heard about this before? (News, current events, school, etc....)*

After Reading: Comprehension and Extension Activity

"After Reading" strategies provide an opportunity to summarize, question, reflect, discuss, and respond to text. After reading the book, work on the following questions with your child or students to check their level of reading comprehension and content mastery.
1. *Why do divers risk their lives to dive so deep? (Summarize)*
2. *Why would a diver go on a volunteer rescue? (Infer)*
3. *How can deep water affect a diver's mind? (Asking Questions)*
4. *What would you explore if you were a deep sea diver? (Text to Self Connection)*

Extension Activity
Water pressure is something you can see for yourself. Have an adult help you poke holes in a tall, empty plastic bottle about two inches (51 millimeters) apart. Fill the bottle with water. Watch the water drain through the holes. You should see the water coming from the top land close to the bottle, and the water from the bottom land farther out. The water pressures from the top to the bottom of the bottle create these differences. Just like deeper diving creates more pressure because of all that water pushing down and around a diver.

TABLE OF CONTENTS

BREATHING UNDERWATER IS TRICKY

It's deep! It's dark! It's dangerous! The deep sea is a **perilous** place. But deep sea divers are driven by curiosity, despite the danger.

☢ **perilous** (PER-uhl-uhs): dangerous

Deep Sea Dangers

A diver has to be prepared
for the unexpected.
Threats include equipment
failure, sea creatures, and
breathing difficulties.

SEA CREATURES THINK YOU'RE DINNER

A shark cage can protect divers, but only if they stay inside. One ocean photographer left his dive cage. A great white shark attacked him. He barely escaped to tell about it.

Whale sharks are the world's
largest fish. They are usually gentle.
But one diver got a little too close.

The whale shark sucked her into its mouth head first. Lucky for her the shark wasn't hungry. It spit her out.

A stingray is loaded with deadly venom. Its long barb is like a **bayonet**. A diver can easily be stung if they get too close.

⚛ **bayonet** (BAY-uh-net): a weapon with a long, sharp blade

Tragic Accident

Famous explorer Steve Irwin was stabbed in the heart by a stingray in 2006. Steve didn't panic. But the wound was fatal.

A squid's fierce bite could **amputate** a hand. A group of Humboldt squid attacked an oceanographer off the coast of Mexico. The squid dislocated his shoulder and broke his hand in five places.

☢ **amputate** (AM-pyuh-tate): to cut off

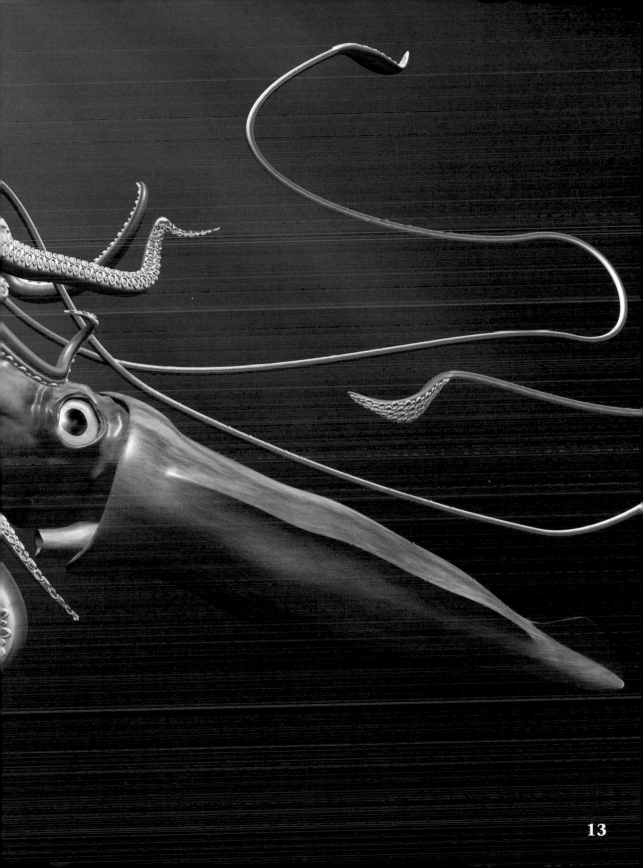

The world's smallest box jellyfish is the size of a thumbnail. Its **toxin** is 100 times stronger than a cobra's. Some divers don't survive the sting.

 toxin (TAHK-sin): a poisonous substance produced by an animal or plant

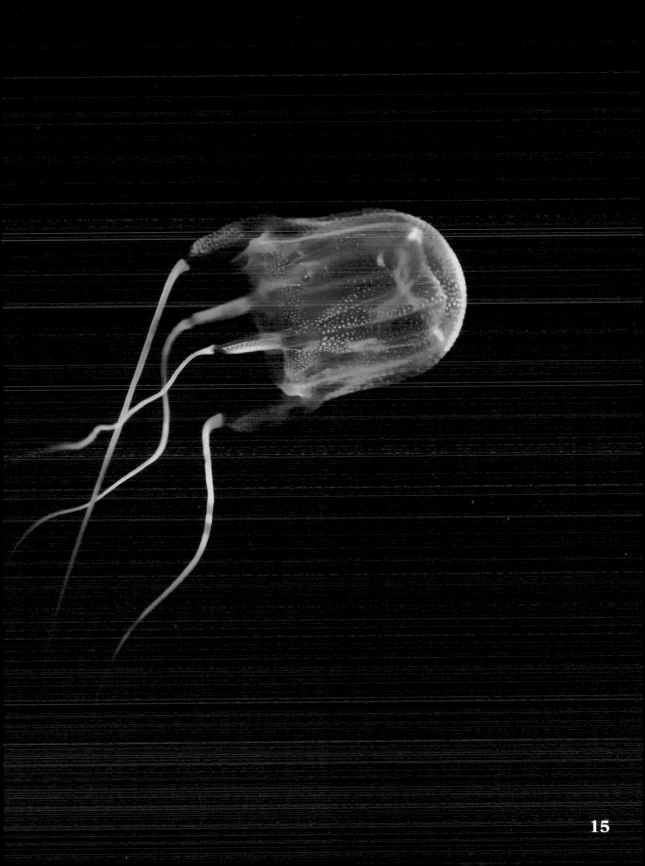

DANGERS LURK EVERYWHERE

Cocos Island off the coast of Costa Rica is one of the most dangerous dive sites. A tiger shark attacked a tourist there. She didn't survive.

Many dangerous dive sites are
so deep that divers suffer nitrogen
narcosis. At Egypt's Blue Hole,
divers get confused and lose their
way back up. More than 150 divers
have died there.

☢ **narcosis** (nahr-KO-suhs): dazed, confused,
or unconscious state

In 2018, a soccer team was stranded in a water-filled cave. Experienced divers led them out. One experienced diver, a Thailand Navy SEAL, died during the mission.

Cave Diving

In a cave, a diver can't
just return to the surface
if they have a problem.
They have to navigate their
way through treacherous
passages first.

Even well-trained, healthy divers can run into trouble in cold, murky waters. They can become **disoriented**. They may experience dangerous changes in their thinking such as hallucinations and paranoia.

☢ **disoriented** (dis-OR-ee-uhnt-uhd): lost, confused, can't figure out which direction to go

At Devil's Ear Cave in Ginnie Springs, Florida, one vortex hits divers with the force of an opened fire hydrant.

Danger Signs

Many Devil's Ear Cave passages are marked with skull and crossbones.

Shipwrecks fascinate divers.
Divers risk their lives for treasure.
In 2007, a 19th century ship, *Nuestra Señora de las Mercedes*, was discovered. It had coins worth 500 million dollars.

Andrea Doria Wreck Still Killing Divers

Andrea Doria sank in 1956. Since then, at least 16 divers have died exploring the deep-sea wreckage.

The Twilight Zone is a region hundreds of feet below the ocean's surface. There, divers collect rare fish using tiny decompression chambers. Most people would never see these creatures if daring divers didn't risk death to discover them.

MEMORY GAME

Can you match the image to what you read?

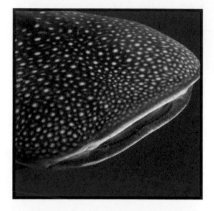

INDEX

SHOW WHAT YOU KNOW

1. What are some reasons divers want to explore deep-water areas?
2. What are some creatures a diver might see in the deep sea?
3. What are some dangers of deep sea diving?
4. What do divers find in the Twilight Zone?
5. Why is it especially dangerous to dive in a cave?

FURTHER READING

Mara, Will, *Deep Sea Exploration: Science, Technology, Engineering*, Scholastic, 2015.

Montgomery, Sy, *The Octopus Scientists,* Houghton Mifflin Harcourt, 2015.

Nye, Bill and Mone, Gregory, *Jack and the Geniuses in the Deep Blue Sea*, Abrams, 2017.

ABOUT THE AUTHOR

Sherry Howard loves the beauty and mystery of the ocean. She once dove into the deep ocean off the coast of Hawaii where she quickly learned to appreciate the dangers. She has tremendous respect for divers brave enough to explore far beneath the waves. She dreams of living on a beach someday.

Meet The Author!
www.meetREMauthors.com

www.rourkeeducationalmedia.com

PHOTO CREDITS: Cover: ©Thomas Bang Photography; page 5, 8-9, 26-27: ©Tammy616; page 6: ©ByronD; page 11: ©aetb; page 11b: ©everett collection; page 12: ©Bun_visit; page 13: ©Paul Fleet; page 14: ©tobynabors; page 15: ©UserG115667539; page 17: ©divepic; page 19a: ©quics; page 19b: ©mihtiander; page 21: ©EXTREMEPHOTOGRAPHER; page 23: ©Placebo365; page 24: ©Valerijs Novickis; page 29: ©Pavaphon Supanantananont

Edited by: Keli Sipperley
Cover and Interior design by: Rhea Magaro-Wallace

Library of Congress PCN Data

Deep Sea Divers / Sherry Howard
 (Daring and Dangerous)
  ISBN 978-1-64369-069-8 (hard cover)
  ISBN 978-1-64369-070-4 (soft cover)
  ISBN 978-1-64369-215-9 (e-Book)
Library of Congress Control Number: 2018955864

Rourke Educational Media
Printed in the United States of America,
North Mankato, Minnesota